Understanding
TEMPTATION

The War Within Your Heart

MARK E. SHAW

CONTENTS

INTRODUCTION

"The widest thing in the universe is not space; it
is the potential capacity of the human heart. Being
made in the image of God, it is capable of almost
unlimited extension in all directions. And one of the
world's worst tragedies is that we allow our hearts
to shrink until there is room in them for little beside
ourselves."[1]

A.W. Tozer

A.W. Tozer penned these thoughts in an effort to get to the "root
of the matter"[2] in examining our own hearts. But can you ever
understand your heart and why you do the things you do? What
about this complicated world of motives, desires, and passions that
exists within what is called the human heart? Is it incomprehensible?

Jesus addressed the heart frequently because He was
concerned about the motivations of His followers. In Matthew
7:17, Jesus taught that outward actions reveal whether a heart is
born again or not: **So, every healthy tree bears good fruit, but
the diseased tree bears bad fruit.** Today, when people sin they
joke that "the devil made me do it" and even followers of Christ
sometimes give Satan more credit than he deserves. Satan is a real
threat, yet Jesus taught that our own hearts are the primary source
of all sorts of wickedness: **And he said, "What comes out of a
person is what defiles him. For from within, out of the heart
of man, come evil thoughts, sexual immorality, theft, murder,
adultery, coveting, wickedness, deceit, sensuality, envy, slander,
pride, foolishness. All these evil things come from within, and
they defile a person"** (Mark 7:20-23). Your heart may not be your
friend but an enemy. The following quote from an ancient Chinese
military general warned about the dangers of not knowing one's
enemy:

---

1 Tozer, A.W. *The Root of the Righteous*, p. 63.
2 Ibid, p. 2.

"If you know the enemy and know yourself, you need not fear the result of a hundred battles. If you know yourself but not the enemy, for every victory gained you will also suffer a defeat. If you know neither the enemy nor yourself, you will succumb in every battle."[3]

What this general did not realize is that our own hearts are our main enemy; they are one and the same.

Without a careful evaluation of our own heart, we can begin to think we are just fine. It can be overwhelming to take a close look at how often we respond wrongly to life's stressors and temptations, and how far off we may be in searching our own heart's motives, but there is hope. God has not left us alone to grovel in the dark trying to figure it all out by ourselves. He has provided His Word and the Holy Spirit to convict us of our heart desires when they go astray (Hebrews 4:12). God has also provided the perfect example in the life of His Son, Jesus Christ, and the body of Jesus Christ—the Church—to provide accountability, fellowship, and opportunities to grow spiritually. Most of all, God promises to give us a new heart and a new nature once we are truly "born again" (see John 3:3; 2 Corinthians 5:17; Ezekiel 36:26; 2 Timothy 1:14).

In this booklet, we will see how Jesus Himself confronted Satan by getting to the "root of the matter" in which he was being tempted. In like manner, we can find victory over sin and temptation when we know our own specific sinful tendencies, the power of the enemy within, and what the Tempter uses to tempt us. Knowing our enemy's plan of attack can prepare our hearts to map out a strategy for overcoming temptation and living in a way that glorifies Christ alone.

A NEW HEART

I love God's promise to the Israelites in Ezekiel 36:26: **"And I will give you a new heart, and a new spirit I will put within you. And**

---

3 Sun Tzu, *The Art of War*, 512 B.C.

I will remove the heart of stone from your flesh and give you a heart of flesh." Understood in its biblical context, this promise addresses the Israelites' wicked, unclean hearts that led them away from God and His goodness:

> **I will take you from the nations and gather you from all the countries and bring you into your own land.²⁵ I will sprinkle clean water on you, and you shall be clean from all your uncleannesses, and from all your idols I will cleanse you. ²⁶ And I will give you a new heart, and a new spirit I will put within you. And I will remove the heart of stone from your flesh and give you a heart of flesh. ²⁷ And I will put my Spirit within you, and cause you to walk in my statutes and be careful to obey my rules. ²⁸ You shall dwell in the land that I gave to your fathers, and you shall be my people, and I will be your God. ²⁹ And I will deliver you from all your uncleannesses. And I will summon the grain and make it abundant and lay no famine upon you** (Ezekiel 36:24-29).

Like Israel, we have to recognize the wickedness of our own hearts and the need for God to gather us (vs. 24), cleanse us from our idols (vs. 25), provide us with a new heart (vs. 26), place His Spirit within us to carry out His will (vs. 27), and grant us a new place to dwell with God (vs. 28). You and I have the same needs as the people of Israel. We are no different. We need God to gather us into His family through the gracious gift of salvation, to cleanse our idolatrous heart desires through sanctification, and to provide us with new heart motives and biblical goals. We need God's Holy Spirit within us to illuminate and empower us to say "no" to sin and "yes" to obeying God's will, and ultimately to grant us a new dwelling place with God forever in eternity.

Recognizing the need for a new heart is the first step in the process of change. If you are a born-again believer, God has provided you with a new heart and that means three things:

- You <u>have been</u> transformed from the kingdom of darkness into the kingdom of light

- You <u>are being transformed</u> into the image of Christ

- You are on your way to <u>ultimate transformation</u> eternally in full and complete glory to come

The emphasis of this booklet is the "being transformed" aspect of Christianity—the fact that after we have been born again, you and I still need God's transforming grace as we are being conformed to the image and likeness of Jesus Christ (Romans 8:29, 12:2). Getting saved is not the final cure for Christians. Salvation is the path to eternal life, but God has a purpose for us and work for us to do. It is rare that God saves the Christian and then immediately calls him to Heaven to a new home as Jesus did for the thief on the cross. More often, God calls the Christian to live on planet earth as an ambassador representing Christ to those who are lost and in danger of going to hell at any moment. God wants the believer in Christ to be transformed (Romans 12:2) by His grace and changed into the image of Christ. Ephesians 5:7-8 warns about partnering, or agreeing with those who are still in darkness, and encourages the new believer in Christ to walk in the light: **Therefore do not become partners with them; for at one time you were darkness, but now you are light in the Lord. Walk as children of light . . . .**

Many books have been written about this topic of being united with Christ and having our identity entrenched in His righteousness. In this booklet however, our focus will simply be these two truths:

1) Everyone needs a new heart.

2) Everyone needs God to cleanse their heart motives to transform them into the image of Christ in order to help a lost and dying world.

We were saved to be messengers of God to save others who are enslaved by life-dominating sin.

One more passage that reminds us of where we came from (sin) and our new identity (righteous in Christ) is found in 1 Corinthians 6:9-11: **Or do you not know that the unrighteous will not inherit the kingdom of God? Do not be deceived: neither the sexually immoral, nor idolaters, nor adulterers, nor men who practice homosexuality, nor thieves, nor the greedy, nor drunkards, nor revilers, nor swindlers will inherit the kingdom of God. <u>And such were some of you</u>. But you <u>were</u> washed, you <u>were</u> sanctified, you <u>were</u> justified in the name of the Lord Jesus Christ and by the Spirit of our God** (emphasis added). Notice the words that I have emphasized. The verb is past tense because that was the identity of the lost person and it is no longer the new identity of the believer. This is an important teaching to remember as we diagnose the heart, because God has empowered us to overcome the enslaving power (not just the righteous penalty) of our sin.

TEMPTATIONS OF THE HEART

Here is the bad news: facing temptation is a lifelong struggle, even if you are a believer trusting in Christ alone. Therefore, it is crucial to diagnose the sinful tendencies in your heart. But the good news is that God has provided everything you need to battle the temptations of this world. Ephesians 6:10-17 details the armor that God has provided to help us: **Put on the whole armor of God, that you may be able to stand against the schemes of the devil. For we do not wrestle against flesh and blood, but against the rulers, against the authorities, against the cosmic powers over this present darkness, against the spiritual forces of evil in the heavenly places. Therefore take up the whole armor of God that you may be able to withstand in the evil day, and having done all, to stand firm. Stand therefore, having fastened on the <u>belt of truth</u>, and having put on the <u>breastplate of righteousness</u>, and, as <u>shoes for your feet, having put on the readiness given by the gospel of peace</u>. In all circumstances take up the <u>shield of faith</u>, with which you can extinguish all the flaming darts of the evil one; and take the <u>helmet of salvation</u>, and the <u>sword of the Spirit</u>, which is the word of God . . .** (emphasis added).

Now, let's look more closely at the nature of temptation.

WHY WE ARE TEMPTED TO SIN

Adam and Eve were created perfect and they lived in a perfect place, but ever since they sinned in the Garden of Eden in Genesis 3, mankind has been tempted to disobey God and His Word. Because of their original sin, everyone else is born with a fallen nature (Genesis 5:3). We are all tempted to live independently from God as if we are "little gods," but we are not. We are created in the image of God but fashioned to depend upon Him in humble submission to His Word. In this section, we want to look at the connection point between our willful heart desires and the emptiness of what the enemy, who is Satan, has to offer in this temporary world. Satan simply wants us to live for this life rather than eternity.

It all began in Genesis 3 in a conversation between the Tempter (Satan) and Eve. Satan offered her a seed of skepticism about what God said and she chose to believe it. He wanted Eve to doubt God's Word and to trust in herself, which she and Adam both did as recorded in Genesis 3:6: **When the woman saw that the tree was good for food, and that it was a delight to the eyes, and that the tree was desirable to make *one* wise, she took from its fruit and ate; and she gave also to her husband with her, and he ate.** The Tempter directed her to focus on pleasing herself. She seized the moment and chose the fleeting pleasures of this world rather than obeying Christ.[4]

Satan used three basic tactics to tempt Eve. 1 John 2:15-17 restates these temptations in this way: **Do not love the world nor the things in the world. If anyone loves the world, the love of the Father is not in him. For all that is in the world, the lust of the flesh and the lust of the eyes and the boastful pride of life, is not from the Father, but is from the world. The world is passing**

---

4 I purposely chose to use "Christ" here (instead of God the Father) to emphasize to our generation that Christ Jesus was there in the beginning of creation according to Genesis 1:26 and John 1:3. He had not yet become man, but He was there.

away, and also its lusts; but the one who does the will of God lives forever. All the world has to offer us can be summarized in these three descriptions: the lust of the flesh, the lust of the eyes, and the boastful pride of life. These are the connection points that you have with the world—the fleeting pleasures offered by Satan in this temporary world. Anytime you and I are tempted to sin, we have experienced either one or more of these same three fleshly desires. Adam and Eve were no different than we are today—whether we are seeking to feed an "addiction" or seeking any type of pleasure. These three temptations have to do with the lies that feed our fleshly desires:

- We can do what we want (lust of flesh)

- We can have what we want (lust of eyes)

- We can be what we want (pride of life)

Commercial advertising today demonstrates how the world aggressively promotes these lies in a variety of ways, and how people are buying into them. Eve was tempted to please the lust of her flesh (Genesis 3:6a, good for food), the lust of her eyes (Genesis 3:6b, a delight to the eyes), and the pride of life (Genesis 3:6c, was desirable to make *one* wise). You and I are tempted in all three ways, too.

Let's take a look at these three messages the world sends us. Should we follow this worldly wisdom? Is it even true? The world says, "You can do whatever feels good to you," but that is not true because you cannot do whatever you want when you live within the parameters of a lawful society. While our culture promotes the "do whatever you want" message, the truth is that it cannot happen; chaos will result. It is the wrong message to send to anyone, especially our young people. Following this message will only leave us empty and dissatisfied. The writer of Ecclesiastes summarizes how his pursuit of pleasure in all its forms turned out for him. He said it was just as vain as **striving after wind** (Ecclesiastes 2:1-11).

Our culture also encourages us to sin in a second way: "You can have anything you want!" This lust of the eyes temptation can never be fulfilled because people often want to obtain possessions or something that God has not granted them. The lust of the eyes is simply a temptation to possess what one sees and thinks will be satisfying to them.

The third lie that tempts our flesh is what the Bible calls the pride of life. "You can be anything you want to be" is a common message, but in fact, this is untrue also. Not everyone can run for President of the United States, become the CEO of a big corporation, or accomplish great things in the field of sports, due to real physical limitations of a wide variety. Not everyone has the mental capabilities to be the President, the skill set required to be a CEO, or the athletic ability to be a sports star. You simply cannot be anything you want to be! The boastful pride of life is fueled by the desire to be like God and to accomplish your will regardless of the consequences. It is a pursuit of accomplishment so that others esteem you highly.

All three of these temptations of the flesh are rooted in the pride of a **haughty** look of the **eyes** (Proverbs 6:17) which is why we must all maintain a humble mindset that accepts only what God wants us to do, what God wants us to have, or what God wants us to be. We are not the Creator but the creation. We are not owners but simply stewards, or managers, of what He owns and has given to us and that includes our abilities. To live "in the flesh" as the Bible says, is to fulfill our own selfish desires. To live "in the flesh" is to live as a "god" of our own lives and is an idolatrous heart problem.

OVERCOMING THE TEMPTATIONS OF THE FLESH

Galatians 5:16-17 reveals the path of overcoming temptations of the flesh: **But I say, walk by the Spirit, and you will not carry out the desire of the flesh. For the flesh sets its desire against the Spirit, and the Spirit against the flesh; for these are in opposition to one another, so that you may not do the things that you please.** The Lord does not want you to **do the things that you please** in regard to your flesh; instead, He wants you to begin to desire the things that please Him (2 Corinthians 5:9) and He gives you the power to do just that.

There is a war inside us between our flesh and the Holy Spirit who lives within us, but God's power is able to conquer our desires according to Philippians 2:13 which says: **for it is God who is at work in you, both to will and to work for *His* good pleasure.** As Christians, we have a new passion in our hearts fueled by the new Person living within us. We are to guard our hearts according to 1 Timothy 2:14: **Guard, through the Holy Spirit who dwells in us, the treasure which has been entrusted to you.** If you choose to obey the temptations of your flesh, then you will quench the Holy Spirit of God (1 Thessalonians 5:19). Temptations to sin will occur because they are everywhere, but the real enemy is within us. In those moments when we give in to the temptation to please ourselves in spite of the consequences, we are taking the easy way and fulfilling our fleshly heart desires.

Every time we give in to temptation, we make it easier to say yes the next time. We need to determine our level of commitment to living out the principles of Scripture that define walking by the Spirit.

One easily identifiable sin in our world today is the sin of drunkenness. The world says certain people are hopeless "addicts"[5] who are riddled with a disease where relapse is the norm. The hopeless state of an addict is a half-truth because all people are hopelessly enslaved to sin prior to experiencing the transforming power of Jesus Christ. "Hopeless" is not just the state of "addicts;" it is true for all unbelievers. The world's deceiving message labels some behaviors "compulsive," which then renders a person victim to something that has overtaken him and can never be resisted. Worldly thinking has no power, no Holy Spirit, and no Savior to offer anyone; therefore, people are led to believe that they are powerless and unable to say no to the temptations of the flesh. Christians must

---

5 "Addiction" is in quotation marks because it is an unbiblical word that the world uses. This term points people to a physical solution for a so-called "disease" which often directs them away from Christ. Biblical words to use instead of "addiction" are idolatry, slavery, sin, and drunkenness. God never calls actions associated with "addiction" a disease in the Bible. Refer to *The Heart of Addiction, (*www.focuspublishing.com) for more details on this principle.

reject worldly words and embrace biblical truth today because we do have the power of the Savior and his Holy Spirit.

> **Now we have received not the spirit of the world, but the Spirit who is from God, that we might understand the things freely given us by God. And we impart this in words not taught by human wisdom but taught by the Spirit, interpreting spiritual truths to those who are spiritual. The natural person does not accept the things of the Spirit of God, for they are folly to him, and he is not able to understand them because they are spiritually discerned. The spiritual person judges all things, but is himself to be judged by no one. "For who has understood the mind of the Lord so as to instruct him?" But we have the mind of Christ** (1 Corinthians 2:12-16).

God's remedy for the Christian is transformation (Romans 12:1-2). Christians must understand that God holds each person responsible to battle the desires of his or her own heart. Even though giving in to temptation brings very real physiological components that feel good to the flesh, we are called to resist them. The physical reward is often difficult to refuse in the moment, especially when the particular pleasure has already been experienced once before. The physical pain of choosing to resist is often not easy to endure either. Choosing to live for Christ in obedience to His Word is hard, but it is possible, and we can only accomplish it by God's moment-by-moment grace. God tells Paul of this grace in 2 Corinthians 12:9: **But he said to me, "My grace is sufficient for you, for my power is made perfect in weakness." Therefore I will boast all the more gladly of my weaknesses, so that the power of Christ may rest upon me.** My prayer is that you will receive hope through the forgiveness of Jesus Christ and the real help found in the Word of God by the power of the Holy Spirit working in you as you apply what you learn in the pages ahead.

OVERCOMING TEMPTATIONS TO SIN

Romans 5:18-21 reminds us of the sad reality of sin and the encouraging truth of the Gospel: **Therefore, as one trespass led to condemnation for all men, so one act of righteousness leads to justification and life for all men. For as by the one man's disobedience the many were made sinners, so by the one man's obedience the many will be made righteous. Now the law came in to increase the trespass, but where sin increased, grace abounded all the more, so that, as sin reigned in death, grace also might reign through righteousness leading to eternal life through Jesus Christ our Lord.** Though Adam and Eve gave in to the temptations of their hearts, we have a model for overcoming sinful temptations and that is Jesus Christ, our Savior and our Model of perfect obedience. Look at the hope found in Hebrews 2:17-18: **Therefore he had to be made like his brothers in every respect, so that he might become a merciful and faithful high priest in the service of God, to make propitiation for the sins of the people. For because he himself has suffered when tempted, he is able to help those who are being tempted.**

Some Christians are unclear about one of the basic goals of Christianity, which is to glorify God by becoming more like Christ as we love God and others. We are His ambassadors (2 Corinthians 5:20; Ephesians 6:20) and God clearly presents the goal to us: become more like Jesus every day for God's glory. God would have us draw near to **the throne of grace** to **receive mercy** and **grace to help** us to change into Christ-likeness in our **time of need.** Our need is to change and grow in our faith in the midst of temptation.

> **Since then we have a great high priest who has passed through the heavens, Jesus, the Son of God, let us hold fast our confession. For we do not have a high priest who is unable to sympathize with our weaknesses, but one who in every respect has been tempted as we are, yet without sin. Let us then with confidence draw near to the throne of grace, that we may receive mercy and find grace to help in time of need** (Hebrews 4:14-16).

11

Jesus conquered sin and death on the Cross as a real human being (fully God and fully human) experiencing pain, suffering and a death that He did not deserve because He was fully obedient. Full of the Holy Spirit, Jesus yielded His will as a man to God's will. In Luke 22:42, He prayed the ultimate prayer of submission saying, **"Father, if You are willing, remove this cup from Me; yet not My will, but Yours be done."** He prayed these words on the night before He was to face separation from God the Father and die a violent death on the Cross. If Jesus Himself prayed this way, then we need to do the same, moment by moment, in our lives, too. Christians have moment-by-moment grace in order to live in moment-by-moment submission. And when we fail, we have the merciful Savior making intercession for us, saying to the Father, "I paid the penalty for that sin too." What a Savior we have in Jesus!

With this hope in Christ and the encouragement to draw near to the throne of grace, turn to Matthew 4 and Luke 4 in your Bible as we walk through the specifics of what Jesus accomplished. It is in these passages that we are told how Jesus Himself overcame the same temptations of the flesh that provoked Adam and Eve to sin, and challenge us today.

LUST OF THE FLESH

Just as Adam and Eve were tempted in Genesis 3a, (food), Matthew 4:1-4 tells us that Jesus was tempted by Satan himself to give in to the lust[6] of the flesh. **Then Jesus was led up by the Spirit into the wilderness to be tempted by the devil. And after He had fasted forty days and forty nights, He then became hungry. And the tempter came and said to Him, "If You are the Son of God, command that these stones become bread." But He answered and said, "It is written, 'Man shall not live on bread alone, but on every word that proceeds out of the mouth of God.'"** Notice the Bible plainly states that Jesus "became hungry" and the fact that He had not eaten for 40 days gives us the degree of hunger He must have felt, but He did not use his fast to justify giving in to this temptation

---

6 For clarification, "lust" simply means "strong desire" and can be applied to any strong desire, not just sexual ones.

of Satan and make himself some bread. Instead, He chose to live in obedience to God's Word rather than His own flesh.

Jesus' desire to satisfy a physical craving of hunger was real, yet He rightly spoke the Word of God and then applied it to His heart and situation. Jesus trusted the goodness of God to provide what He needed at the right time. Jesus was not trusting in His own ability to turn a stone into bread though He could do it. Likewise, as humans, we sometimes have money in our pockets to do what we want and please the lust of our flesh. But God wants us to seek Him by reading and studying His eternal Word, and trusting in His goodness to provide what we truly need now and in eternity. The real rewards are not in this life but in eternity.

Notice that this temptation began with a challenge to Jesus' identity: **And the tempter came and said to Him, "If You are the Son of God . . . ."** In an earlier section, we learned of our new identity found in Christ and that we are united with Him through His righteousness. If you do not recognize this basic biblical truth that you belong to Christ and are buried (Colossians 3:3-4) in Him (meaning you lose your desires and now live to fulfill His desires), then you will always struggle against the attacks of the tempter.

Also notice how Jesus answered using the Holy Scriptures: **But He answered and said, "It is written, 'Man shall not live on bread alone, but on every word that proceeds out of the mouth of God.'"** How important is it to know, study, memorize, and meditate upon the Word of God? The answer is simple: vitally important. If Jesus quoted the Word, you and I must do so, too. Jesus quoted a passage that recognizes the importance of depending upon physical bread to live and yet takes that truth one step further—namely, it is also vital to live upon **every word that proceeds out of the mouth of God**. Do you need food to eat? Yes, of course, and the temptation of Eve in Genesis 3:6a was that the forbidden fruit was **good for food,** so you are often tempted to do something that might look at first that it is necessary for life's sustenance and enjoyment.

Jesus was clearly hungry but He did not turn the stone into bread. He did not satisfy a real, physical craving in a wrong way. Idolatrous desires may be inherently good desires like the one to eat food. There is nothing sinful about eating a meal for sustenance. However, when a good desire becomes something that is a consuming priority, then it becomes idolatrous. God has allowed us to have desires, but He wants us to desire what He wants for us. That is when we will most enjoy what He has approved and it will ultimately glorify Him!

When we give in to the lust of the flesh temptation to fulfill a desire in a wrong way, we are challenging God's goodness, love, and provision. You may not see it that way at first, but since you are bought with a price (1 Corinthians 6:20), you no longer belong to your former masters (Satan and yourself). Christ-followers belong to God who owns them. One of the basic heart motives behind this temptation is rebellion, or living to please self above God regardless of the consequences.

Do not give in to the consuming desire to experience a pleasurable activity above what God has approved. The prideful heart behind this temptation led Adam and Eve to rebel against God and the same thing plagues many pleasure seekers today who secretly say in their hearts, "I want pleasure, and I know I can trust myself to do what is good for me." We have all said, "I know what is best for me," even though God has said differently. Be careful that you do not allow your desires to lead and rule your heart but that you allow God's Spirit and Word to lead and rule your heart: **Guard your heart above all else, for it determines the course of your life** (Proverbs 4:23, NLT).

LUST OF THE EYES

Eve was tempted by what she could see in Genesis 3:6b: **it was a delight to the eyes.** The Bible warns us often about what we put before our eyes (Proverbs 4:25; 2 Corinthians 10:7; 1 Thessalonians 5:22). We are all tempted to live by sight rather than by faith in what cannot be seen. The second temptation Jesus successfully faced was the lust of the eyes depicted in Luke 4:5-8: **And he led Him up and showed Him all the kingdoms of the world in a moment of time. And the devil said to Him, "I will give You all** this domain and its glory; for it has been handed over to me, and I give it to whomever I wish. Therefore if You worship before me, it shall all be Yours." Jesus answered him, "It is written, 'You shall worship the Lord your God and serve Him only.'" This temptation is a desire to possess something that one can see but that God has not given.

Eve saw that the forbidden fruit was **a delight to the eyes** and she succumbed to the temptation but Jesus did not. Instead, Jesus rightly identified that the heart of this temptation was not physical craving but a worship issue. 1 Corinthians 10:31 states: **Whether, then, you eat or drink or whatever you do, do all to the glory of God.** Therefore, all that we do should be designed to glorify God. When we worship Him alone rather than fulfill our own prideful desires to possess something for selfish gain, or because we "just want it," then we will say no to the compelling desire to possess status, a material good, or any temporal (which means temporary or earthly) possession.

In the lust of the eyes temptation, God's omniscience, or perfect wisdom, is challenged by a desire in the heart to trust in one's own best thinking and ideas. "I know what I want, and I must have it" is what someone struggling with this temptation to sin says. It is rooted in the pride of trusting in one's own understanding (Proverbs 3:5-8).

Satan told Eve **"you will not surely die"** as if there would be no consequences even though God had said to Adam in Genesis 2:16-17 that eating from the tree in the middle of the garden would bring forth death. The temptation here promotes an attitude of "serving oneself," but we were created to serve God by loving and serving others as acts of worship. Jesus rightly quoted and applied the scriptural commands to worship God alone and to serve Him alone. You must do the same: seek to serve God and others, not yourself, in all things.

Think about it in this basic way: the lust of the eyes is all about taking rather than giving. Acts 20:35 states: **In all things I have shown you that by working hard in this way we must help the weak and remember the words of the Lord Jesus, how he** himself said, **"It is more blessed to give than to receive."** A heart living to please self views appealing items with the basic mindset of that of a consumer, or a taker. This same heart struggles to be a giver who uses things to serve God's kingdom and His people. Clearly, a person living as a consumer obtaining what is visible only for selfish gain has a worship disorder because God has called us to give and serve, not seek to be served, just as Jesus modeled before us in Matthew 20:28: **It shall not be so among you. But whoever would be great among you must be your servant, and whoever would be first among you must be your slave, even as the Son of Man came not to be served but to serve, and to give his life as a ransom for many."**

Do not give in to the temptation to possess something God has not given yet or may not ever give you. Guard your heart by carefully trusting the wisdom of God and not what you can see that looks delightful. "Why wouldn't God want me to have this?" or "I know what I must have to make me happy," are statements we make in our hearts when tempted to sin in this way. The pursuit of happiness is strong, and it might even be a way to avoid pain. "Shop-a-holics," as they are called by the world, fall into temptation because they mistakenly believe they must possess things in order to be happy. A young woman caught in this snare might regularly go shopping, spending money she does not have, because she is unhappy in her marriage and seeking to avoid the pain of her situation. She may have an eye for making things beautiful and think everything she sees "needs" to go into her living room. She has a compelling urge to possess things regardless of the consequences. Haven't we all wanted things God has not given?

THE PRIDE OF LIFE

The third temptation that Jesus faced is called **the boastful pride of life** in 1 John 2:16 (ESV). Eve was further tempted in Genesis 3:6c to eat the fruit because it was **desired to make one wise**. The pride of life is a desire to be what we want to be. Persons who struggle with this temptation put God to the test instead of allowing Him to accomplish His purposes and plans for their lives. Because he was fully a man, Jesus was tempted in Luke 4:9-12 just as we are to fulfill the desire to be wise: **And he led Him to Jerusalem and had Him stand on the pinnacle of the temple, and said to Him, "If You are the Son of God, throw Yourself down from here; for it is written, 'He will command His angels concerning You to guard You,' and, 'On *their* hands they will bear You up, so that You will not strike Your foot against a stone.'" And Jesus answered and said to him, "It is said, 'You shall not put the Lord your God to the test.'"**

The desire to receive praise and attention from others is one prideful root in the heart of this temptation. God's omnipotence, or power, is challenged by this temptation to make much of ourselves as we might say inwardly: "I trust myself. I can be whatever I want. I can take care of this myself." Me, me, me. The heart attitude here fails to recognize God as sovereign and almighty and chooses to live as though he or she is all-powerful and self-sufficient. You may often see this in a very competitive person who achieves great things because he is driven to succeed by the accolades of mankind. Also, people-pleasers struggle greatly with this temptation because they desire the praise of others.

Jesus was not insecure, nor was His aim to please man. He knew His identity and who He was. More importantly, He knew the Father. Jesus was seeking only the approval of God the Father. He accomplished the will of His Father rather than the will of mankind, or even His will as a real human person.

In the Old Testament, the Israelites put the Lord God to the test at Massah in Exodus 17:1-7:

> **Then all the congregation of the sons of Israel journeyed by stages from the wilderness of Sin, according to the command of the Lord, and camped at Rephidim, and there was no water for the people to drink. Therefore the people quarreled with Moses and said, "Give us water that we may drink." And Moses said to them, "Why do you quarrel with me? Why do you**

test the Lord?" But the people thirsted there for water; and they grumbled against Moses and said, "Why, now, have you brought us up from Egypt, to kill us and our children and our livestock with thirst?" So Moses cried out to the Lord, saying, "What shall I do to this people? A little more and they will stone me."

Then the Lord said to Moses, "Pass before the people and take with you some of the elders of Israel; and take in your hand your staff with which you struck the Nile, and go. Behold, I will stand before you there on the rock at Horeb; and you shall strike the rock, and water will come out of it, that the people may drink." And Moses did so in the sight of the elders of Israel. He named the place Massah and Meribah because of the quarrel of the sons of Israel, and because they tested the Lord, saying, "Is the Lord among us, or not?"

Psalm 95 refers to this Exodus 17 moment when the Israelites tested the Lord God in their unrighteous anger. Psalm 95:6-11 contrasts the heart fueled by the pride of life in a willful, rebellious sinner with the heart submitted to the will of the Father:

Come, let us worship and bow down, Let us kneel before the Lord our Maker. For He is our God, and we are the people of His pasture and the sheep of His hand. Today, if you would hear His voice, do not harden your hearts, as at Meribah, as in the day of Massah in the wilderness, "When your fathers tested Me, they tried Me, though they had seen My work. For forty years I loathed *that* generation, and said they are a people who err in their heart, and they do not know My ways. Therefore I swore in My anger, Truly they shall not enter into My rest" (NASB).

Does God hate sin? Yes. Why? Because it does not glorify Him and it brings relational separation between mankind and God. In the passages above, God was providing for them and He had not forgotten them though they were thirsty, angry, and experiencing real suffering.

Isn't it interesting that one of the final teachings Jesus gave to His disciples in Matthew 26:41 had to do with temptations? **Keep watching and praying that you may not enter into temptation; the spirit is willing, but the flesh is weak.** Peter and the disciples were sleeping rather than praying. Today, Christians are doing whatever they want regardless of the Word, and they are spiritually sleeping rather than praying and depending upon almighty God. When this occurs, they are putting the Lord to the test.

Though Satan quoted Scripture in Luke 4, he misinterpreted and misapplied the Word and he did not fool Jesus. Jesus rightly interpreted and applied Scripture to His situation and we must do the same thing. We must read, study, memorize, and meditate upon the Bible to have a kingdom mindset that will glorify God and not our own glory or pleasures. God will have it no other way, because He will not share His glory with any created being. We were designed to glorify Him alone and not ourselves.

The Bible warns in Deuteronomy 6:16-19: **You shall not put the Lord your God to the test, as you tested *Him* at Massah. You should diligently keep the commandments of the Lord your God, and His testimonies and His statutes which He has commanded you. You shall do what is right and good in the sight of the Lord, that it may be well with you and that you may go in and possess the good land which the Lord swore to *give* your fathers, by driving out all your enemies from before you, as the Lord has spoken.**

When you seek to know God and to submit to His will by doing what is right according to the Scriptures, your temptations to sin will decrease, and you may even overcome your enemies by His power.

The temptation of the pride of life is within all of us, and we are warned just as the Israelites were in Deuteronomy 8:17-20: **Beware lest you say in your heart, "My power and the might of my hand have gotten me this wealth." You shall remember the Lord your God, for it is he who gives you power to get wealth, that he may confirm his covenant that he swore to your fathers, as it is this day. And if you forget the Lord your God and go after other gods and serve them and worship them, I solemnly warn you today that you shall surely perish. Like the nations that the Lord makes to perish before you, so shall you perish, because you would not obey the voice of the Lord your God.** If this is a problem for you, let me urge you to stop playing around with a desire to be something important. If you know your identity is in Christ, you are as important as you need to be and God gives you your worth.

Since we are created in the image of God, we sinfully desire to be like God and to receive the praise and attention of others. Do not trust your self-sufficiency and God-given abilities to accomplish goals that do not line up with the Holy Scriptures. God is not sharing His glory with anyone and the prideful heart will be humbled. In other words, the prideful heart will be humiliated and brought low. Clearly, God is concerned with one priority and that should be your priority as well: His glory.

STAGES OF SIN AS APPLIED TO "ADDICTIONS"

In many of my writings I seek to address the heart of what the world calls "addiction." In these three temptations, I often witness a progression of sin that is not only true of the so-called "addicts" but all believers. Here is an example of a chemical addiction described through the progression of different stages of sin:

A young woman tries an alcoholic beverage and enjoys the buzz. She begins drinking alcohol as often as possible when it makes sense to do so, because it is fun (lust of the flesh). She enjoys the taste and the social time with friends. It begins to be something that she looks forward to and then lives for. In other words, she makes it a priority in her life (which the Bible would call 'worship' when that priority supersedes God). She begins placing this desire for alcohol and fun ahead of other priorities such as her family responsibilities, job tasks, time with non-drinking friends, church, and most importantly, her relationship with God in prayer and Bible reading. Many of those who love her begin to see that her love of drinking alcohol has become idolatrous desire so they intervene by confronting her with the truth in love. But now she says that she "must have a drink" to feel normal and enjoy life (lust of the eyes). Drinks have become like possessions. Actually, she likes to get drunk as much as possible now. The state of drunkenness has become a possession to her that once was fun but now has become her main thought and goal each day (a so-called obsession). In fact, she would have to admit, "This is who I am" as it is who she has become. Partying, drinking, and all that the lifestyle of drunkenness brings has become part of her identity (pride of life). She does not hide her drinking as she first did and is rather proud to be known as a party animal.

While that example may seem extreme at first glance, I would urge you to consider that it is not as far-fetched as many would believe. Having counseled so many people who are enslaved to "addictions" over the years, this is a fictional story based upon many counselees. Sadly, it is too familiar to me now.

The same sin progression can be described for the angry man: He enjoys being angry at others. It makes him feel good (lust of the flesh). He begins to think, "I must act this way toward others in order to avoid the pain of being hurt myself." The possession he longs for is to have people take note of his opinion so hurting others is the way his voice is heard and how he protects himself. Being angry is beginning to be his identity to those who know him (pride of life). He is enjoying the attention he is receiving as an angry man and how others are intimidated by him.

You can see how this could be the same sin progression for those who struggle with depression and do not wish to change, or gamblers enslaved to greed, and to many other life issues where a person's most identifiable character trait is the sin that is so evident to others and often blind to self. That is why examining the heart is so important because this new identity is what many in biblical counseling refer to as life-dominating sin, and in the Bible, God labels the fool, the angry man, the drunkard, thief, adulterer, and idolater by their sin when they have voluntarily given themselves over to such a pattern of living.

The progression of sin in our hearts is not as complex as it appears. God's Word and the Holy Spirit reveal our heart motives according to Hebrews 4:12-13: **For the word of God is living and active, sharper than any two-edged sword, piercing to the division of soul and of spirit, of joints and of marrow, and discerning the thoughts and intentions of the heart. And no creature is hidden from his sight, but all are naked and exposed to the eyes of him to whom we must give account.** The hope in these verses is that God knows each of our hearts. He is revealing our sinful heart desires to us so that we can change and begin to experience victory. No longer victims of our sin-enslaved heart, we are victors by God's grace and mercy and are capable of **putting off** sin and **putting on** true righteousness found in Jesus Christ:

> **But that is not the way you learned Christ!—assuming that you have heard about him and were taught in him, as the truth is in Jesus, to put off your old self, which belongs to your former manner of life and is corrupt through deceitful desires, and to be renewed in the spirit of your minds, and to put on the new self, created after the likeness of God in true righteousness and holiness** (Ephesians 4:20-24).

Ahab was a king of Israel in the days of the prophet Elijah. As king he had everything anyone could possibly desire. But when he saw his neighbor's vineyard he wanted it for himself (lust of the eyes). He went to Naboth, the owner of the land and said, "Give me your vineyard, that I may have it for a vegetable garden." (1 Kings 21:2) But Naboth told him he could never give up the "inheritance of my fathers." 1 Kings 21:4 records Ahab's reaction to this denial of his desire: **And Ahab went into his house vexed and sullen**

because of what Naboth had said to him, and he lay down on his bed and turned away his face and would eat no food.

Ahab's wife, the wicked Jezebel, was more than happy to appeal to his flesh and pride: "Are you not the king?" she asked (pride of life). "I will give you the vineyard of Naboth," (lust of the flesh) she said in 1 Kings 21:7. Thereafter, she put in place an elaborate scheme that would end the life of Naboth and secure for Ahab the coveted vineyard. Verse 16 records Ahab's reaction: **And as soon as Ahab heard that Naboth was dead, Ahab arose to go down to the vineyard of Naboth the Jezreelite, to take possession of it.**

Over and over in Scripture we see examples of what happens when our fleshly lust conceives a desire in our heart giving birth to evil (James 1:15). The Apostle Paul warns us against even approving of the works of our flesh birthed in darkness (Ephesians 5:11) and commands us to stay alert to the tactics of the enemy that tempt our flesh by admonishing us to walk **as children of light,** bringing glory to God whose light we represent. Now, let's look at the put-on attitudes and behaviors that please God as they are the antidotes to the three sinful heart desires: lust of the flesh, lust of the eyes, and pride of life.

THE ANTIDOTES

An antidote for a poison is a substance that counteracts the negative effects on a person who might otherwise die. Since our old sin habits are still in our flesh, God has provided His antidote to fight the toxins that tempt us.

Recall that Satan appeared to Eve in the Garden as a serpent. Later, God used the form of a bronze serpent on a pole as the antidote to the poisonous bites the Israelites were experiencing during their 40 years in the wilderness. Numbers 21:5-9 records how the people grumbled and sinned against God, complaining to Moses about their circumstances:

And the people spoke against God and against Moses, "Why have you brought us up out of Egypt to die in the wilderness, for there is no bread or water, and we detest this worthless food."

So the Lord sent poisonous snakes among the people, and they bit the people; many people of Israel died. Then the people came to Moses and said, "We have sinned, for we have spoken against the Lord and against you. Pray to the Lord that he would take away the snakes from us." So Moses prayed for the people. The Lord said to Moses, "Make a poisonous snake and set it on a pole. When anyone who is bitten looks at it, he will live." So Moses made a bronze snake and put it on a pole, so that if a snake had bitten someone, when he looked at the bronze snake he lived.

Don't miss the lesson here: The bronze serpent is an Old Testament type of Jesus Christ who was "made sin for us." **Just as Moses lifted up the serpent in the wilderness, so must the Son of Man be lifted up, so that everyone who believes in him may have eternal life** (John 3:14-15). The solution for a sinful heart will not come from within one's own flesh but from without: from Jesus Christ and His power.

There are similarities and overlapping themes in these three particular types of temptation. All of them are rooted in pride, trust of self, idolatrous desires, receiving glory for self, disobedience, doubting God and His character, seeking to please self, avoiding pain, and usurping God's good plan for living found in His Word. While we all struggle in each of these areas, we usually find that we are more challenged with one of them than the others. I noticed a trend when I counseled three men separately but during the same time period for the specific problem of gambling.

- Guy #1 loved to gamble and go to the casino. Win or lose; it was fun!

- Guy #2 loved to gamble because he was focused upon winning some money so he could buy things he could not otherwise afford.

- Guy #3 loved to gamble because he liked to beat the system by betting on teams he had researched extensively, and he liked playing cards with friends to show he was the best.

These three guys all loved to gamble; however, they gambled for three very different reasons. One counseling technique would not work for all three. I had to realize WHY they gambled so I could address their hearts with the right antidote!

Some people struggle with the lust of the eyes more than they do with the pride of life or lust of the flesh. They see things they want and are constantly having to put-off and put-on other desires in their hearts. Others may battle the lust of the flesh and wanting to do what they want to do—now! Take note of which one is your primary sin choice and be aware of it at all times, not neglecting knowledge of the others.

Temptation	Sin Root	View of God	How Eve Was Tempted in Genesis 3	How Jesus Triumphed in Gospels
Lust of the Flesh (to do)	Act on your feelings, appetites, and desires	Doubt God's goodness and love; seek pleasure above all	Genesis 3:6a "good for food"	Matthew 4:1-4 Luke 4:1-4 Jesus chose to obey the Word.

Lust of the Eyes (to have)	Fulfill your selfish and covetous desires	Doubt God's wisdom; worship of self, living for what is seen	Genesis 3:6b "delight to the eyes"	Matthew 4:8-11 Luke 4:5-8 Jesus chose to worship the Father.
Pride of Life (to be)	Exalt yourself to be "like God" receiving praise from others	Doubt God's power and sovereign plan; defy and test God by doing what you want	Genesis 3:6c "desired to make one wise" and "become like God"	Matthew 4:5-7, Luke 4:9-13 Jesus chose to submit His will to match the Father's will despite impending suffering.

You can see in the examples above three of the central heart motives that frequently drive gambling. While some people are tempted in all three ways, others may gamble primarily for only one of the three reasons stated above. Examine your heart. Gathering data by asking yourself questions is important. Consider which of the three temptations are the most challenging to you. Recognize that all three temptations are a struggle for all people, but is there one in particular that plagues your heart? There is no escape from the temptations of this world, but it is possible to overcome them through the Word of God and the Holy Spirit's power to obey the Word.

It is crucial to understand the nature of our rebellious hearts and how we seek to fulfill the lust of the flesh, the lust of the eyes, and the pride of life. And Satan, the enemy of our soul, well knows where we are vulnerable to his tempting attacks. It is imperative that you know yourself; that you are aware of your spiritual weakness so that when you are tempted by his poisonous bites you possess the antidote in the power of victory through the Holy Spirit. The Holy Spirit within you can conquer your heart's desires with God's antidotes.

Let me extend a word of caution here that we guard against establishing our own righteousness and not submitting to the righteousness of God. Each of the following antidotes must be applied with prayer that God will give you the strength you do not have in yourself. Jesus understood our state: **Watch and pray that you may not enter into temptation. The spirit indeed is willing, but the flesh is weak** (Matthew 26:41).

ANTIDOTE FOR THE LUST OF THE FLESH: THE WORD

The antidote for this temptation is simple obedience to the Word of God. God repeatedly commands us to do things that we cannot do apart from His strength and Spirit: love those who persecute you, be kind to your enemies, love your spouse, discipline your children, and do not get drunk with wine are all examples of doing the hard thing that God requires. Perhaps you can think of many more that apply to you personally. So how do you do the hard things that God requires? The answer may seem simple but it is hard to do; you must obey the Word of God by the power of the Holy Spirit of God.

People who enjoy their habitual sin because it is fun must reverse their thinking. The Bible calls this reversal of thought "renewing the mind" and "repentance." 2 Corinthians 10:4-6 describes the method by which we are to employ God's divine power in our battle against the flesh: **For the weapons of our warfare are not of the flesh but have divine power to destroy strongholds. We destroy arguments and every lofty opinion raised against the knowledge of God, and take every thought captive to obey Christ, being ready to punish every disobedience, when your obedience is complete.** Trusting in God and His Word only comes as one learns what God says and implements it in a practical way. James 1:22 tells us: **But be doers of the word, and not hearers only, deceiving yourselves.**

So if you are a gambler, tempted by your own heart's desire to have fun, you must remind yourself that while God is not against fun, He is against fun that leads to destruction. Gambling is poor stewardship of God's money that He has provided to you. He expects you to be a good steward of the blessings He gives you. The truth is that God is the Owner and you are His servant and that must dominate your heart. As you study Scripture—God's Word—His Spirit of truth will be revealed to you. You obey Him (not the other way around) so you do what He says in His Word.

As a biblical counselor, I want to teach my counselees a new way to live: by reading and studying the Word, spending time in prayer, talking to other believers in intimate fellowship and the sharing of heart issues, being counseled even when it involves hearing the hard truth, attending church services to corporately worship Christ, and serving others in a sacrificial manner. I want my counselees to re-define "fun" and find the activities of the Christian life fun to do. I want obedience to Christ to become joyful because it is when one has a Godly perspective and mindset!

ANTIDOTE FOR THE LUST OF THE EYES: WORSHIP

The antidote to the lust of the eyes temptation is worship. Instead of being preoccupied with acquiring things to consume upon self, the person tempted with the delight of their eyes must remember that we were created to worship God. We worship something or someone because we have assigned worth to it, and when that happens, we serve obediently, radically, and sacrificially by giving up personal desires for the ONE who makes life worth living. The drug addict has assigned great worth to the drug he or she pursues relentlessly, and in the end finds emptiness.

The Holy Spirit and God's Word are essential in this antidote. We live in an amazing culture of technology and material goods. The enticing things of the world are constantly within reach for the Christian. The challenge for us is to discipline our frivolous hearts to keep our eyes on Jesus and worship only Him. Everything else is a false idol the enemy uses to snare your heart.

The person who enjoys possessing things they can see must begin to walk by faith as a worshipper of Jesus Christ, trusting in what they cannot see.

If you are tempted by your own heart's desire to possess more things, remember it is God's will for you to worship and serve Him, not yourself through your wants and pleasures. You must recognize areas in your life that need to be radically transformed. You must acknowledge that God is the owner of all your possessions and you are His servant, and that must dominate your heart. The reality is that whatever else you worship will never bring satisfaction, this is found only in God. **As death and destruction are never satisfied, so the eyes of a person are never satisfied** (Proverbs 27:2).

We are warned in Proverbs 4:23 to **keep your heart with all diligence,** by guarding the affections of our heart. Colossians 3:2 states: **Set your affections on things above, not on things on the earth.** We do that by keeping our eyes on the cross of Jesus Christ and worshiping only Him.

ANTIDOTE TO THE PRIDE OF LIFE: THE WILL OF GOD

The last antidote for the temptation called the pride of life is submission to the Will of God out of a desire to glorify Him and not self. Humility is the key. Again, be reminded that God often tells us to do something that we cannot do apart from His strength and the Holy Spirit and that includes obeying the will of God. In Luke 22:42 Jesus was facing separation from God the Father and a violent death on the Cross, and He prayed, **"Father, if You are willing, remove this cup from Me; yet not My will, but Yours be done."** No one can obey God in the struggles of life without God's grace.

If your priority in life and your heart's desire is to be admired by others, you must keep reminding yourself of God's truth that you are created to glorify Him and not yourself. You might be a very gifted person who believes you have accomplished much in your own strength and power, but the truth is that success is from God, and you must submit to God's will and plan for your life. This requires understanding what God's Word says, placing yourself under a Christian yet human authority, and being careful to do only what God has required. We must fight against a heart that desires the praise of men.

When I have counselees who primarily struggle with this temptation, I must teach them about submission, surrender, and obedience. One of the things I say is that "submission always has a human face" which simply means that we submit to another person as unto the Lord. A person who works at a restaurant may boast saying, "I always do what my boss tells me to do," but when asked to clean filthy bathrooms as part of her job says, "I can't do that! Did you see how awful it is in there?" Her reaction demonstrates that she does not have a surrendered heart.

It is interesting to note that the Apostle John in his short letter of First John made an example of Diotrephes, a man who sought to have pre-eminence among the church leaders, and John called him evil (3 John 9-11). We are all like Diotrephes when our heart's desire is to want what we think is best and do what we want to do independently from God. At times, we are all guilty of seeking our own will for our own honor and glory, when that honor and glory is due God alone. He is the Creator and we are His creatures. Nowhere in the Bible does God command men to seek out their own praise and admiration. Be cautious to resist the lure of living independently from God. That is what happens when we submit to the pride of life temptation. Satan would have us believe that we can be the master's of our own fate; free to make our own plans and follow our own desires. The pride inside our hearts leads us to want these things, but God calls us to surrender our will to His will so that He might be glorified in the sight of others.

God wants to be glorified. He wants people to see who He truly is, and He has called us to reveal His character to others. We accomplish that by demonstrating a submitted, trusting heart to a good, wise, and all powerful God who loves us better than we love ourselves.

Temptation	Sin Root	View of God	Antidote
Lust of the Flesh (to do)	Act on your feelings, appetites, and desires	Doubt God's goodness and love; seek pleasure above all	**Word** of God; obeying commands of God rather than one's own feelings
Lust of the Eyes (to have)	Fulfill your selfish and covetous desires to possess	Doubt God's wisdom; worship of self, living for what is seen	**Worship** of God; seeking to serve and please God as an act of worship rather than pleasing self
Pride of Life (to be)	Exalt yourself to be "like God" receiving praise from others	Doubt God's power and sovereign plan; defy and test God by doing what one wants	**Will** of God; submitting one's own will and conforming it to God's will even in adverse circumstances; not desiring the praise of man

CONCLUSION

You have been introduced to three practical ways in which a Christian can counteract a few of the primary temptations of the heart connected to what the world offers. But God does not expect you to accomplish this on your own! By His Spirit, God empowers the follower of Jesus Christ to obey His commands by fulfilling His will and bringing honor to His name. When the Christian does what God says to do in His Word, those obedient choices result in glorifying God. Glorifying God is connected to wise choices. For example, when Joseph was tempted by Potiphar's wife to commit sexual sin in Genesis 39, he said: "How can I do this great evil and sin against God?" and he fled in obedience to God's will. Joseph acted immediately with resolve to avoid the temptation, and we must do the same. Our motive must be to honor God by not sinning against a loving Savior who died to forgive us from our sins, past, present, and future.

Knowing your heart's propensity to find fulfillment in something other than God is the beginning of the battle, but obeying Him is the end of the battle. While fleeting, idolatrous heart desires exist in the flesh of every believer, there is a moment of choice between pleasing self or pleasing God, whereby one either follows the flesh or the Spirit's leading. In time, your desires within the flesh can be replaced with worshipful obedience to the Word by doing the will of God that ultimately results in the transformation of your heart's desires. The promise is that as you practice godliness in your obedience, you will be transformed (Romans 12:1-2) by God's amazing grace and become more Christ-like.

1 John 4:4 provides the follower of Jesus Christ with a tremendous promise of victory: **Little children, you are from God and have overcome them, for he who is in you is greater than he who is in the world.** By God's grace, might, and indwelling of the Holy Spirit (1 Timothy 1:14), you are empowered by God to obey His Words for the purpose of glorifying Him. As a Christian, you may still wrestle with your own heart desires, but you are not without hope because of the One who lives inside of you. Trust in Christ as you obey God and walk in His truth.

Truly, for the rest of our lives, we are going to be tempted by our prideful desires to do, to have, and to be. None of us are exempt from these temptations of the flesh, and we will all be tempted by all three of these worldly heart motives. The natural progression of sin can develop a stronghold, or pattern of sin habits in our lives that is not easily broken. But God has not left us powerless! We must pray and ask God to apply His spirit of Truth at times of our temptation in very practical ways. The indwelling of the Holy Spirit empowers us to surrender and obey the Word of God. God has provided what the Christian needs to overcome any desire of the flesh.

Remember the goodness, wisdom, and power of God is greater and much better than your own goodness, wisdom, and power. Do not be easily tempted by the temporary pleasures, possessions, and power the world and Satan offers us all. God alone is worth your temporary sacrifices in this life. God's love for you can be trusted because He can be completely trusted. He alone is worthy of all praise and glory forever. Amen.

Do not love the world or the things in the world. If anyone loves the world, the love of the Father is not in him. For all that is in the world—the desires of the flesh and the desires of the eyes and pride of life—is not from the Father but is from the world. And the world is passing away along with its desires, but whoever does the will of God abides forever.

1 John 2:15-17

APPENDIX I
PRACTICAL TOOLS

1. LUST OF THE FLESH

   A. Identify your feelings and thoughts about what your flesh desires to do. Compare them with biblical truths. If you do not know the Bible well, journal those feelings and thoughts and ask a Trusted Christian Friend (TCF) to help you find biblical truths to combat those feelings and thoughts when they are sinful.

   B. This may sound extreme but do NOT trust yourself. In the beginning of your walk with Christ, you can assume that your desire is to please your own flesh. Think of it simply as your default like a computer has a default font. This will allow you to pause and examine your heart motive. Then you can ask yourself, "What do I want? What am I seeking?" If your motive is not selfish, then praise the Lord. If it is, then you have time to correct it. Assume the worst about your heart because it might not be your friend.

2. LUST OF THE EYES

   A. Identify your feelings and thoughts regarding what you are seeing and longing to possess. Ask yourself: "What is it about this item that I think is going to satisfy me? Why do I want to possess it so much?" Again, a TCF might be necessary to ask you these questions and more in order to identify potential idolatrous heart desires.

   B. Assume your desire to possess is likely selfishly motivated. This will allow you to pause and examine your heart motive by asking yourself, "What do I want? What am I seeking?" If your motive is not selfish, then praise the Lord. If it is, then you have time to correct it.

3. PRIDE OF LIFE

   A. Identify your thoughts and feelings regarding what you desire to be. Ask yourself questions like: "What do I perceive in myself that I lack? Do I want others to admire or approve of me?" You may need a TCF to point out that you are struggling with that particular desire in the first place and then to help you identify why those particular struggles are occurring in your heart.

   B. Assume you are probably acting in certain ways because you desire the praise and approval of others. It may be the kind of car you choose to drive, the clothes you wear, and other things you do that are motivated by a pride of life desire to be noticed, envied, admired, or approved by others. Examine your heart and do not assume the best about your motives. After evaluating your motives, if you find that they are not selfish at the root, then praise the Lord. If they are selfishly rooted, then repent and humble yourself before God to be what He has called you to be in Christ.

Books and Booklets by Mark Shaw

Books

The Heart of Addiction
    Workbook
    Leader's Guide
Relapse: Biblical Prevention Strategies
Divine Intervention: Hope and Help for Families of Addicts
Addiction-Proof Parenting
Cross Talking: A Daily Gospel for Transforming Addicts
Eating Disorders: Hope for Hungering Souls
Strength in Numbers: The Team Approach to Biblical Counseling

Booklets

Hope and Help through Biblical Counseling
Hope and Help for Sexual Temptation
Hope and Help for Gambling
Hope and Help for Self-Injurers and Cutters
Hope and Help for Marriage
Hope and Help for Husbands and Fathers
Hope and Help for Video Game, TV, Internet "Addiction"
The Pursuit of Perfection (with William Hines)
Understanding Temptation: The War Within Your Heart